HOOKWELL'S SCHOOL

Captain Hookwell

(and Blackbeak)

Mr Mallick

Colin Bootleg

Josh Cutler

Carlos Fernandez

Erin Flint

Han Hopkins

Amber Stormbrow

Chapter 1

Josh Cutler loved being at Hookwell's School. It looked like a ship, it had a moat with a toothless shark, and hammocks for every pupil to sleep in. But there was one big problem. Hookwell's School was for the children of pirates and his mum was a pilot. If the head teacher, Captain Hookwell, found out, Josh would be expelled. Only his best friends Amber, Han and Carlos knew his secret.

One morning, Josh's class were in their cabin waiting for their teacher, Mr Mallick, to arrive. The door burst open and a pirate sprang through.

HOOKWELL'S SCHOOL FOR PROPER PIRATES 4

Written by Jan Burchett and Sara Vogler

Illustrated by Jack Viant

RISING ★ STARS

Hachette UK's policy is to use papers that are natural, renewable and recyclable products and are made from wood grown in well-managed forests and other controlled sources. The logging and manufacturing processes are expected to conform to the environmental regulations of the country of origin.

ISBN: 9781398325418
Text © 2021 Jan Burchett and Sara Vogler
Illustrations, design and layout © Hodder and Stoughton Ltd

First published in 2021 by Hodder & Stoughton Limited (for its Rising Stars imprint, part of the Hodder Education Group), An Hachette UK Company, Carmelite House, 50 Victoria Embankment, London EC4Y 0DZ
www.risingstars-uk.com

Impression number 10 9 8 7 6 5 4 3 2 1
Year 2025 2024 2023 2022 2021

Author: Jan Burchett and Sara Vogler
Series Editor: Tony Bradman
Commissioning Editor: Hamish Baxter
Illustrator: Jack Viant/Bright Group International
Educational Reviewer: Helen Marron
Design concept and page layout: Gary Kilpatrick
Editor: Amy Tyrer

With thanks to the schools that took part in the development of Reading Planet KS2, including: Ancaster CE Primary School, Ancaster; Downsway Primary School, Reading; Ferry Lane Primary School, London; Foxborough Primary School, Slough; Griffin Park Primary School, Blackburn; St Barnabas CE First & Middle School, Pershore; Tranmoor Primary School, Doncaster; and Wilton CE Primary School, Wilton.

A catalogue record for this title is available from the British Library.

Printed in the United Kingdom.

Orders: Please contact Hachette UK Distribution, Hely Hutchinson Centre, Milton Road, Didcot, Oxfordshire, OX11 7HH.
Telephone: (44) 01235 400555. Email: primary@hachette.co.uk.

MIX
Paper from
responsible sources
FSC™ C104740

He had a mean look on his face and waved a gigantic hook.

"You are my prisoners!" he snarled.

The class got ready to fight, but the pirate grinned and whipped off his hook. He had a real hand underneath.

"Only joking!" he said.

He wrote his name on the board. "I'm Mr Blaze," he announced.

"Where's Mr Mallick?" asked Carlos.

"He's gone to dance in the Pirate Jig Competition," said Mr Blaze.

The class cheered. It was Mr Mallick's dream to win that competition.

"He'll be back next week," said Mr Blaze. "Now, what's our pirate mission for today?"

Everyone yelled at once.

5

"Gymnastics," suggested Han.

"Pirate martial arts," said Amber.

"Inventing new school dinners," called Josh.

"Great suggestions," said Mr Blaze, writing them on the board. "We'll take a vote ..."

The door opened and Captain Hookwell strode in. Blackbeak, her pet parrot, sat on her hat.

"Ahoy shipmates," she boomed.

"Ahoy Captain," yelled the pirates.

"I see you're having fun with your new teacher," said the captain.

"Shipmates, I have a challenge from Captain Squint!"

Everybody booed.

Squint was the head teacher of Grabbit School for Pirates, and Captain Hookwell's sworn enemy.

"Squint wants a pirate gymnastics competition here tomorrow," the captain went on. "And no pirate refuses a challenge."

"It's number seventy-seven in the Pirate Code," said Carlos.

"It will be four against four," said Captain Hookwell. "He says our team must be Han, Carlos, Amber and Josh. He's never forgotten the sea monster you set on him or how you escaped from his prison. Squint wants revenge."

"No chance!" said Amber.

"We have our mission, shipmates," said Mr Blaze. "Outside, class, and we'll make the gymnastics course."

"Aye aye!" said the class, grabbing their pencils and exercise books and rushing out to the yard.

In no time, Carlos had written a plan.

"We use the wrecked boat on the beach and add some extras," he explained. "The contestants ..."

"That's us," said Amber.

"... do cartwheels around the edges, handstands on barrels in the centre, backflips over the oars, then swing from the mast into a net."

"I can't wait for the competition," said Han, when the boat was finished. "My mum will be proud. She was the best gymnast when she was a pupil here."

"She's not the best shot though," grinned Carlos.

Han's mum, Hotshot Hopkins, was in charge of the school cannon. She never hit her target.

"My great-great-great-great-grandmother, Speedy Stormbrow, was the world's fastest pirate swimmer," said Amber.

"Wow!" said Josh.

"It was only because a shark was chasing her," said Amber.

"I wish my family were pirates," said Josh.

"What did you say?" said a voice.

Erin stood there with her friend Colin. Erin disliked Josh and wanted him expelled from Hookwell's School. What had she just heard?

Chapter 2

"Er ... I said I wish my family were pirate swimmers," said Josh in a rush.

"I don't think they are pirates at all," said Erin. "I'm telling Captain Hookwell."

"And I'll tell Captain Hookwell that you haven't helped with the gymnastics course," said Han.

Colin looked scared. "She'll tell the captain we hid in the trees and didn't do any work," he said.

"Shut up, Colin," snapped Erin.

She stormed off with Colin scampering after her.

That evening, Josh's friends rushed off to tea. Josh wasn't in a hurry. It was pilchard pie and ginger custard.

As he passed Captain Hookwell's cabin, Mr Blaze sneaked out!

He was wiping ink from his fingers.

"Ahoy, sir," said Josh.

Mr Blaze quickly wrapped his inky fingers in his hanky.

"Just planning a surprise for the captain tomorrow," he whispered as he hurried away.

Mr Blaze isn't just a great teacher, thought Josh. *He's kind too.* He couldn't wait to see what the surprise was.

But then he thought about the expression on Mr Blaze's face. *Could he have been doing something bad?*

The next afternoon, the whole school marched outside for the gymnastics competition.

The yard was covered in everything that the class had invented. There were beams balanced on barrels and monkey bars made from anchors. There was a springboard with a giant treasure chest to jump over. And at the end stood their wrecked boat with its nets, barrels and ropes.

"Attention, shipmates," said Captain Hookwell. "We don't like Grabbit School, but we'll follow the Pirate Code. If we lose in a fair competition, we will accept our defeat." Then she grinned. "But we're going to win! Good luck, shipmates."

Squint's ship arrived at the jetty. Squint and the Grabbit School pirates burst out of the ship and charged up to the school.

"I don't think you can trust him," Blaze muttered to Josh and his friends.

Squint glared at Josh and his shipmates. "You're going to lose," he sneered.

"We'll see about that," said Captain Hookwell. "May the best school win."

"That's us," said Squint, stuffing a gigantic muffin into his mouth. "My team will go first."

13

Four Grabbit pirates stepped up to the starting line.

Captain Hookwell blew her whistle and turned over her egg timer. The Grabbit pirates set off. They wobbled along the beams, fell off the monkey bars, crashed into the treasure chest and had a fight on the boat.

Finally, they all limped over the finishing line.

"Twelve minutes," announced Captain Hookwell.

"We'll beat that easily," declared Amber.

"Wait a minute," said Mr Blaze. "I reckon those Grabbits are cheats. I'll check they haven't meddled with the course."

Mr Blaze took his time checking the equipment.

Then he gave a thumbs-up.

Captain Hookwell blew her whistle, turned over her egg timer and Josh and his friends set off.

14

Josh sprang on to a balance beam, but the top was slippery. He skidded along and tumbled off the end. The anchors came loose as Amber tried to swing along them and the springboard snapped as Carlos landed on it. Only Han was still going. She leapt on to the wreck.

"Look out!" yelled Josh.

The wrecked boat creaked and fell apart. Han jumped clear just in time.

"You've had more than twelve minutes," screeched Squint, snatching the egg timer. "You've lost!"

Chapter 3

"Grabbit School has cheated," shouted Captain Hookwell. "They did something to the course."

"Nonsense," said Squint smugly. "You know what happens now you've lost. Check the Pirate Code."

"You're wrong, Squint!" said Captain Hookwell. "There's nothing in the Pirate Code about gymnastics competitions. I'll fetch the code from my cabin and show you."

92. No Pirate cheats another Pirate

93. Any school that loses a Pirate gymnastics competition is taken over by the winners!

Captain Hookwell was soon back with a scroll.

"Look here," she said as she unrolled it. "There's nothing in the code ..." Her expression changed. "Shiver me shipwrecks! It's at the very bottom.

Any school that loses a pirate gymnastics competition is taken over by the winners!"

"Hookwell's School is ours!" yelled Squint.

Josh was horrified.

Captain Hookwell was shaking with anger. Then Josh caught sight of Mr Blaze's grin.

Suddenly he knew exactly what had happened.

"It's not in the Pirate Code," he called out. "Mr Blaze wrote it on the scroll last night."

"Rubbish!" shouted Squint. "You lot never stop trying to spoil things for me."

"I saw him sneaking out of Captain Hookwell's cabin," said Josh. "He had ink on his fingers and he tried to hide it. He's on Squint's crew."

"That's right, Josh," said Mr Blaze. "And not one of you worked it out until now."

"But that's cheating," shouted Amber.

"No pirate cheats another pirate, Squint," bellowed Captain Hookwell. "Take your pupils and go!"

"Grab them, Grabbits," shouted Captain Squint.

Before the Hookwell's teachers knew what was happening, the Grabbit pupils threw a net over them and tied a rope tightly around it. Squint's pet eagle, Scar, circled above.

"Let me out, you hopeless herrings," wailed a voice from under the net.

"You were supposed to get out of the way, Captain Squint," called a Grabbit pupil.

"I knew that," said Squint, as Mr Blaze pulled him free.

"My brilliant plan worked," he said. "I invited Mallick to a pretend jig competition."

"And I captured him and took his place," boasted Mr Blaze. "It's all been so easy. Nobody even saw what I did to the gymnastics course."

"You won't get away with this," shouted Captain Hookwell.

"I will," sneered Squint. He turned to his crew. "Lock these snivelling teachers up."

"The basement has a storeroom with a strong lock," said Blaze.

"Throw them in there with Hookwell's parrot," said Squint, "and bring me the key."

The friends watched their teachers being marched away.

"We must rescue them," whispered Josh, "and fight to get our school back."

"And quickly," said Han.

Mr Blaze came back with a large key. "I've put Mallick in there too," he said.

Squint hung the key on his belt. "This won't leave my side," he said. "Listen up, all you Hookwell's pupils. You're our servants now. You'll be cooking and scrubbing. And anyone who misbehaves will be cleaning the toilets with their toothbrush."

The Grabbits cheered.

Chapter 4

That night, Josh huddled with his friends in a corner of the hall. All the other Hookwell's pupils were asleep on the cold floor.

"I'm so hungry," whispered Han. "It was horrible watching those nasty Grabbits eating our tea."

"It's not fair," said Amber angrily. "They're sleeping in our hammocks too."

"No talking," said a voice from the wall.

"Who's that?" said Josh.

"Squint," said Carlos. "He's put speaking tubes all over the school so he can hear what's going on. We must whisper."

"Our mission – free our teachers, now!" whispered Amber.

"Let's slip out," whispered Han. "We can creep to the captain's cabin and get the key when Squint's asleep."

They jumped up.

"What are you doing?" demanded Erin from the other side of the hall. Colin was snoring beside her.

"Just a bit of exercise before bed," said Josh. They quickly did some push-ups.

It was ages before Erin fell asleep.

They tiptoed to the hall door and Josh opened it a crack.

"Blaze is out there," he hissed.

"We'll just have to carry out our mission tomorrow," said Carlos.

Early the next morning, a shrill whistle blasted down the speaking tube.

Everyone woke with a start.

22

"Attention, you lazy lobsters," came Squint's voice. "I've written a list of your jobs."

Mr Blaze flung open the door and hammered a list to it.

"Read this," he barked. "And get to work." He strode away.

"We're on deck-scrubbing duty," Carlos said to the others, pointing to the list. "Every single floor has to be scrubbed."

"At least we're not cleaning the toilets," said Amber.

"But we won't have time to get the key," said Han, frowning.

"Wrong!" said Josh. "Our new job is perfect. We'll scrub the captain's cabin first.

FEED SCAR
EAT MUD
SHINE BOOTS
CLEAN CABINS
SCRUB DECK
CHOP ONIONS
(NO GOGGLES ALLOWED)

I'll get Squint's attention while one of you sneaks the key from his belt."

They grabbed a mop, brushes and a bucket of water and made for the captain's cabin.

Carlos knocked on the cabin door.

"Who's there?" shouted Squint.

They marched in.

Squint was sitting in Captain Hookwell's chair, gobbling up his breakfast kippers.

Scar was on Blackbeak's perch. The giant eagle peered at them with her beady eyes.

Josh had saved Blackbeak from Scar once. He knew how much Captain Hookwell adored Blackbeak.

"Deck inspection team, sir," said Han. "Making sure your floor is squeaky clean, sir."

"We're following your orders, sir," said Josh.

He quickly slopped some water on the floor and they began scrubbing.

The cell key was hanging from Squint's belt. Josh nodded to Amber and dropped his mop with a clatter.

"Stop that noise!" yelled Squint.

Amber stretched out a hand. Her fingertips were almost touching the key.

Suddenly, Scar gave an angry screech.

Chapter 5

Squint was so surprised he jumped to his feet. His boot plunged into the bucket, spilling water everywhere. He tried to pull it out, staggered backwards and sat down on his kippers. His face turned bright red.

"Get out!" he bellowed.

Josh and his shipmates sat in the hall, eating their breakfast of chewed crusts that the Grabbits had left.

"We nearly got the key," said Han. "What's our new plan of action?"

But just then, Erin and Colin marched up to their table.

"Captain Squint is going to have a flag raising ceremony," said Erin. "Everyone outside."

"Everyone outside," echoed Colin.

"Who are you to give us orders?" demanded Amber.

"I've decided to join Squint's crew," said Erin. "I'm fed up with sleeping on the floor and eating chewed crusts."

"You sneaky seaworm!" said Josh.

"Wait until I tell Squint that you're not from a pirate family, Josh!" said Erin. "He'll kick you out."

"Squint won't care," said Josh. "As long as I scrub the floors."

Erin stormed off, Colin scuttling behind her.

Everyone headed outside for the ceremony. Splinters of wood and shredded rope lay all over the yard.

The Grabbits had wrecked the gymnastics course.

"A big pirate cheer for the new head teacher of Hookwell's School," yelled Mr Blaze from the roof.

The Grabbits cheered as Squint burst out of the door.

His boot squelched and kippers were stuck to his bottom. His pupils sniggered.

"Silence!" he shouted. "Pull down Hookwell's flag."

Josh and his shipmates could hardly watch as Mr Blaze tore down their flag.

Then he hoisted the Grabbit School flag. It was a picture of Squint.

Mr Blaze fired the cannon in celebration.

Squint jumped in terror, lost his balance and fell in the moat.

Gums, the toothless shark, came to have a look at him. Squint screamed.

"This is our chance," said Josh. "We'll help him and get the key at the same time."

They ran to the moat where Squint was trying to escape from Gums.

They grabbed his collar and pulled. As Squint lay gasping on the ground, Carlos's fingers inched towards the key on his belt.

Suddenly Erin was there. "I'll look after him," she snarled.

"What a horrid accident, Captain Squint," she said sweetly, wrapping him in a blanket. "Let's go to the kitchen and get you a cream bun."

"Two cream buns," whimpered Squint. "And a nap in my cabin."

Erin and Colin led him away.

"If it hadn't been for them ..." snarled Amber.

"I can't believe they've joined Squint's crew," said Han crossly.

"Forget about them," said Carlos. "I have a new plan. Once Squint is asleep, we climb through his window and get the key."

"I'll go," said Josh.

He sneaked around the outside of the school, reached the captain's cabin and peeped in.

Squint was asleep in his hammock.

Josh rattled a window but it wouldn't open.

"Go away!" Squint screamed. "You're dead!"

Josh froze. Had Squint seen him?

But Squint was curled up in terror, his eyes tightly shut. "Don't hurt me, Deadly Doris," he yelped.

He let out a gigantic snore.

He's dreaming, thought Josh and that gave him an idea. He sprinted back to his friends.

"Squint was dreaming about someone called Deadly Doris," he said. "He sounded terrified."

"Grandma Stormbrow used to scare us with stories of her," said Amber. "Every pirate on the Seven Seas feared her and her razor-sharp cutlass."

"I have a plan," said Josh. "Deadly Doris is going to haunt Squint tonight."

Chapter 6

"But Deadly Doris does not haunt Hookwell's School," said Carlos.

"She will tonight," said Josh. "We'll dress up in a fake ghost costume and appear to Squint."

"Brilliant," said Amber. "She'll tell him to hand over the key and leave the school."

"Hookwell's School will be ours again," said Josh.

"But we can't leave the hall," said Carlos. "Mr Blaze will be on lookout."

"Oh yes we can," said Han.

That night, Han, Josh, Carlos and Amber crept out of the hall, carrying mops.

"Where do you think you're going?" snapped Mr Blaze.

Han pretended to be frightened.

"Please sir," she said, her lip trembling. "We didn't finish scrubbing our class cabin."

"Can we have permission to go and do it now?" asked Josh.

"You lazy pirates," barked Mr Blaze. "Get on with it and don't come back until you're finished!"

"Our class cabin will have everything we need to make the ghost," whispered Han as they hurried along.

They reached their cabin and stopped in shock.

"The Grabbits have wrecked it," gasped Carlos.

CAPTAIN HOOKWELL LOST!!

DOWN WITH THE HOOKWELL PIRATES!

The Grabbits had torn up the exercise books and ripped the maps off the wall. They'd covered the lanterns in seaweed.

"We have to get our school back before they wreck it completely," said Amber. "Let's make that costume."

"We'll use a sail," said Han.

"Perfect," said Josh, pulling one down from a shelf.

"What was Deadly Doris like?" asked Carlos.

Amber thought hard. "Grandma said she was very tall," she said.

"I'll sit on your shoulders," Han told her.

"She had wild, straggly hair," said Amber.

Josh put his mop on Han's head.

"That won't do," said Amber. "Her head was cut off!"

"Oh dear," said Josh. "Hang on ... I'll stick my head under Han's arm."

They stitched the sail into a spooky ghost shape, cutting holes for the arms and head.

Han climbed on Amber's shoulders and Josh draped the ghost costume over them.

Josh scrambled under the sail and stuck his head out. Carlos plonked the mop on top of it.

"One more thing," he said.

He rushed into the class stockroom and came back with a tin of green paint.

He slapped it all over Josh's face.

"Excellent," he said, holding up a seaweed-covered lantern. "More scary than Deadly Doris herself!"

The ghost wobbled along the passage to the captain's cabin.

Squint lay in his hammock, fast asleep. Scar was on Blackbeak's perch. She opened her beady eyes.

Josh screwed up his face into a terrifying expression and let out a horrible moan.

"Who's there?" whimpered Squint, peeping over his blanket.

The ghost wobbled up to his hammock.

"It's Deadly Doris!" wailed Josh. "You have been a bad pirate, Squint. You have broken the Pirate Code."

"Go away," whimpered Squint.

"I will haunt you forever," said Josh.

"No!" howled Squint.

"There's only one way to stop me," hissed Josh.

"I'll do anything," whispered Squint.

"Give me the key to the storeroom," wailed Josh. "And leave Hookwell's at once."

Squint held out the key with trembling fingers.

Grabbing the key, the ghost wobbled and staggered for the door.

But the sail caught on the door knob. There was a loud rip and the sail fell to the ground.

Squint stared in shock at Josh's green face and Han sitting on Amber's shoulders.

"I knew it!" he screeched. "Give me back that key!"

"Run!" yelled Han.

They dashed along the passageway and down the stairs to the storeroom.

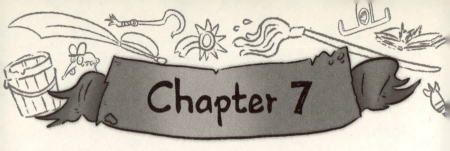

Chapter 7

Han unlocked the storeroom door.

The teachers burst out, Blackbeak flapping over their heads. Mr Mallick high-fived the friends. Han hugged her mum.

"Nice work, my brave shipmates," said Captain Hookwell. "How did you get the key? And why is Josh green?"

Carlos quickly told her the whole story. "Squint and his crew won't give up without a fight," he said.

"We'll see about that," said the captain.

She led the charge up the stairs and burst into the school hall. All her pupils ran to her side.

Then Squint marched in, his crew behind him. Captain Hookwell strode up to him. Scar and Blackbeak glared at each other from their captains' hats.

"Get out, Squint," growled Captain Hookwell.

"Never!" screeched Squint. "Hookwell's School is mine. Grabbits, attack!"

The Grabbits rushed forwards. Josh grabbed a mop from the broom cupboard and tripped up the enemy as they came for him. Carlos and Amber stood back-to-back and stuck their smelly feet under the Grabbits' noses.

Han and her mum grabbed buckets and rammed them over the heads of any Grabbits that came near.

Pressed up against the tall deck at the front of the hall, Josh kicked free and scrambled up onto the deck.

As the enemy rushed up, he poked the first one in the chest with his mop. They tumbled down like dominoes. Mr Mallick was dancing a fast jig, dazzling the Grabbits and bopping them on the head with a wooden leg.

Captain Hookwell was chasing Squint.

Blaze snatched a loop of rope and swung it in the air.

He was after Captain Hookwell! Josh threw his mop at a picture high up on the wall. It crashed down over Mr Blaze's head and he slumped to the ground, trapped in the frame.

Blackbeak whooshed past Josh's nose. He whizzed round Scar in tight circles until the eagle screeched in terror. Erin was rolling Colin along the ground, knocking Grabbits over. Erin had decided to be loyal to Hookwell's School again!

We're winning! thought Josh. He pushed more Grabbits down the steps.

Suddenly, Captain Hookwell's commanding voice cut through the air.

"Stop fighting, shipmates," she yelled. "We surrender!"

Chapter 8

Josh didn't understand. Why was Captain Hookwell surrendering?

Then he spotted Squint. Squint had his hands around Blackbeak's neck.

"That's right, you snivelling sea-snakes," sneered Squint. "Stop fighting or Scar will have the parrot for dinner."

Hookwell's pirates surrendered.

"Now you're the ones who have to leave," sniggered Squint. "And I will keep Blackbeak. If you want him to stay alive, you will never return to Hookwell's School."

"I agree," said Captain Hookwell sadly.

Josh suddenly saw a trapdoor under his feet. Before anyone spotted him, he ducked out of sight and slipped through.

He dropped down into a room lit by a small porthole.

He squeezed through and found himself out by the moat. Somehow, he had to sneak back into the school and rescue Blackbeak. There was an open porthole high on the wall with a drainpipe close by. Josh was terrified of climbing up high. But it was his only hope of freeing Blackbeak and saving his school.

Josh began to climb the drainpipe. He reached the porthole and looked down into the hall.

A sad line of Captain Hookwell's pirates was being marched out of the door.

Squint was barking orders, his hands still around Blackbeak's neck. Scar was eyeing the parrot greedily. Josh slipped through the porthole and crawled along a beam. He didn't dare look down. He caught hold of a rope, swung over Squint's head and let go. He landed on Squint's back, ramming his hat down tightly over his eyes.

Squint gave a shriek and let go of Blackbeak. Josh jumped to the floor.

Blackbeak swooped away to perch on Captain Hookwell's hat.

The captain turned. The Hookwell's School pirates turned.

The Grabbits took one look at their angry faces and fled.

"Wait for me," squealed Squint, stumbling about blindly.

Carlos pushed him out of the door, and Squint tumbled into the moat!

The Hookwell's School pirates all cheered.

"You saved our school!" yelled Carlos.

"We all did," said Josh.

"But you were amazing," said Han.

Josh realised he could face even the tallest mast now.

"Excellent work, Josh!" said Captain Hookwell. "We'll have a celebration for my four brave buccaneers and invite your parents."

Josh felt a stab of fear. If his mum came, Captain Hookwell might discover the truth.

45

Chapter 9

It was the day of the celebration. Josh, Han, Amber and Carlos proudly wore their gold pirate medals. Josh looked round to find his mum. He could see Erin and Colin in the corner, scrubbing the floor as punishment for helping Squint.

Oh no! Erin had spotted Josh's mum and was talking to her. Erin gave Josh a horrible smile.

"I knew I was right," she said. "Your mum isn't a pirate. She's a pilot."

"Your mum isn't a pirate?" Captain Hookwell had heard every word.

"No," Josh said sadly. He had a sinking feeling in his belly.

"Hookwell's School is for the children of pirates," said the captain.

Josh felt terrible. He was going to have to say goodbye to his friends and to pirate school.

"However, you are very brave," Captain Hookwell went on. "You saved our school even though you were in danger. Josh Cutler, you are a proper pirate and I really want you to stay at Hookwell's School."

"Aye, aye, Captain," said Josh happily.

Amber, Han and Carlos high-fived Josh.

"Let's celebrate with fish paste ice cream," said Amber.

Josh grinned. The food might be rubbish, but Hookwell's School was brilliant!

Chat about the book

1 Go to Chapter 6. How had Amber's grandmother described Deadly Doris?

2 Read page 25 and 26. Why was Amber unable to get the key from Squint?

3 What was Josh's problem at the beginning of the story? How was this problem resolved by the end of the story?

4 How does your opinion of Mr Blaze change in the story?

5 Go to page 40. Why did the author say, 'They tumbled down like dominoes'?

6 Erin and Colin had to scrub the floor because they helped Squint. Do you think this was a fair punishment?